I WANT TO BE A
TEACHER

Written by
Valerie Poh

Edited by
Jonathan Reule

Illustration
Phan Quỳnh Trang

Storyboard
Keziah Gan

UNIBINO
B O O K S

First paperback edition October 2023
ISBN 978-981-17359-7-4

Published by Unibino Pte. Ltd.
9 North Buona Vista Drive, #02-01 Metropolis Tower 1, Singapore 138588

www.unibino.com

Teachers are the backbone of our modern world. They're great in helping us to learn new information, push our minds beyond what we already know, and even inspire us to keep going when times are tough. If you ask your parents or even grandparents about the teachers in their lives, it's almost certain they have at least one teacher who has made a big impact on them!

But why are teachers so special and what exactly do they do to make such a lasting impression on our lives? Teachers are often some of the first adults we are entrusted to, other than our family members. They often have big hearts and a love for helping to guide others.

Now, how about you? Do you enjoy sharing information you've learned with your friends and family members? Do you ever jump in to help a friend when they're struggling to understand a concept - or find it rewarding when you can teach a younger sibling ideas you already know?

If you find yourself saying yes to many of these questions, then you might be the right fit to be a teacher one day! But of course, being a teacher requires more than just wanting to help others. There are basics skills you need to learn and programs that you'll need to attend. However before we jump into that, why don't we first have a look at how this profession formed?

If you were to ask a prehistoric human what a 'teacher' is, they'd probably stare back at you, slack-jawed, and confused by the term. You might even get some funny looks. But that's not to say that our early ancestors weren't already well acquainted with the concept of a teacher.

In fact, there were many teachers back in those days, when we were living in small niche tribes. It was often the elders in those tribes, who'd lived many years, and seen plenty of interesting events during their time, who would help teach the younger generation basic survival skills.

From hunting to fishing, tool making, skinning animals, and even spotting danger before it happens - these elders were more than happy to pass down their wealth of information, to better ensure the survival of the next generation.

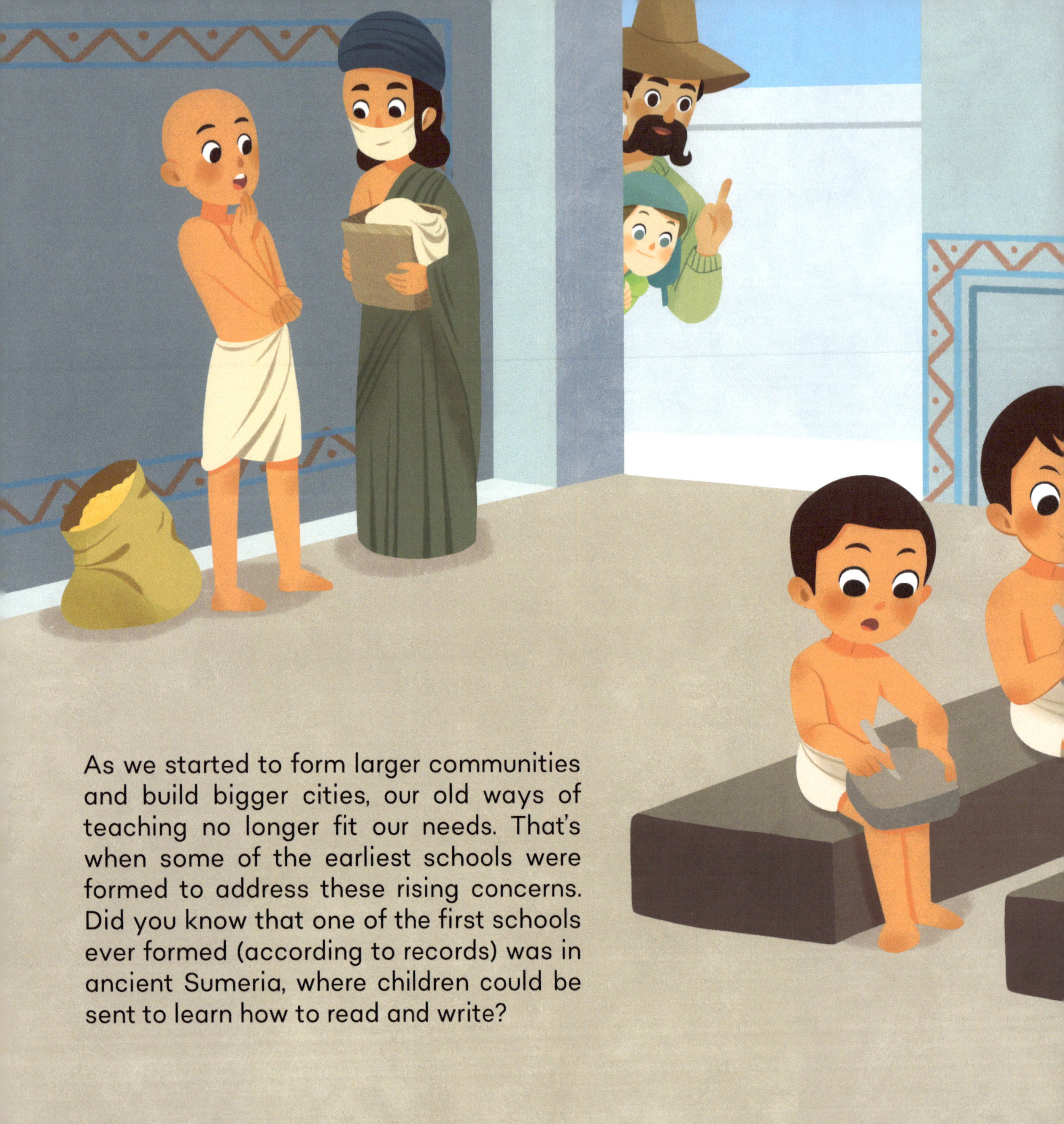

As we started to form larger communities and build bigger cities, our old ways of teaching no longer fit our needs. That's when some of the earliest schools were formed to address these rising concerns. Did you know that one of the first schools ever formed (according to records) was in ancient Sumeria, where children could be sent to learn how to read and write?

These schools in ancient Mesopotamia soon became quite popular, as the children who graduated from them could go on to become a scribe and earn a comfortable living for themselves. Parents were eager to have their children learn reading and writing as the job of a scribe was in high demand throughout Sumeria - they needed plenty of lists and records made. The only downside to this school was that they were often harsh environments, where even the slightest peep could be punished!

If we hop ahead to a place like ancient China we'll see how these schools slowly evolved to incorporate more subjects than just reading and writing. These schools were often led by government officials, who would teach young boys skills such as archery, mathematics, and music, along with other moral virtues like manners and the importance of loyalty.

It's unfortunate that at these times long ago, girls weren't allowed to attend these schools in China. However, they still had their mothers who would take it upon themselves to teach their daughters a basic education in maths, writing, and the duties expected from them by society.

As society progressed into medieval times, having a formal teacher was still a rare occurrence. There were a few reasons for this, the first being how expensive teachers were to hire. The second is that there were no public schools at those times. And the third is that many saw a formal education to be of little use to their children, given the outlook of jobs that were readily available during those times.

There were some places that offered an informal education, such as monasteries and other religious institutions. This education often came in the form of a music school, where children were taught how to sing in church choirs, for Sunday gatherings and other special occasions. In these music schools, children would learn how to read Latin, so they could sing their songs properly, and could also be trained to be Monks - who were usually hired as tutors later on in their lives.

If we dig a little deeper into our history, we'll find that teachers have always been around, it's just that they were called by different terms. Since the middle ages relied so heavily on skilled professionals, such as blacksmiths, carpenters, cobblers, leatherworkers, bakers, and many more - there was enough demand for knowledge and expertise in various fields.

And as such, this brought about what was known as apprenticeships. This was an arrangement whereby a master would take an eager mentee under their wing and train them in their area of expertise. These arrangements were quite common back in the late middle ages, and children even as young as 10 could often be sent to live with a mentor, to fulfil their apprenticeship duties and one day become an expert themselves!

Of course, sometimes teachers are called upon not only for their knowledge but also their determination and willingness to help so-called difficult students. If we fast forward to the late 18th century we'll find an exceptional teacher, who took on what many considered an impossible student. Anne Sullivan became famous for how she was able to help a young girl who was both deaf and blind.

Anne worked with Helen Keller, who up until that time, had no understanding of reading or writing, or even how to speak. With a massive amount of patience and ingenuity, Anne was able to reach Helen and taught English, by tracing each letter on Helen's palm and spelling out full words. Within her first day, Helen learned over 30 words after many failed attempts by previous teachers of the past!

Another example of how teachers can make a world of difference comes from a high school teacher in California by the name of LouAnne Johnson. Back in 1989, LouAnne took on a classroom full of at-risk youth, who were disinterested in the materials covered in their schools.

LouAnne persisted in coming up with various ways to engage her students, such as giving karate lessons and even using music lyrics to teach them poetry. She eventually inspired her students to stay in school, and even develop an interest in poetry and literature. Because of her efforts, many of these students graduated High School and left with more than a degree, but self-confidence and a belief in their own abilities.

Now how about teachers in our modern world? Are you curious to see what different professions are available to these hardworking educators? If so, then let's start with the most commonly known: academic teachers. These teachers often educate children to young adults - in either a specific academic subject or a basic level of several foundational subjects.

Being a high-school teacher requires a bachelor's degree in the teaching subject you want to specialise in. You will also need to be flexible and open-hearted, as you will be teaching a range of teenagers. Some may be rebellious, others enthusiastic, while some could need a little extra help and attention. So, it'll be important to be caring and empathetic to many different personalities in your classroom.

Being an academic professor will require you to pursue further education, like a master's and even a doctorate, and you might also need to dedicate several years to research while you teach. The kind of teaching you do will be mostly in the form of lectures, with students in the older age range. Engaging these students would require you to be relatable and it could be helpful to understand current ongoing trends too.

You can also be a special education teacher for students with various learning disabilities, such as developmental delays and physical disabilities. You will typically need a diploma in special education, and having a lot of patience would be helpful, as your students would typically take a longer time to complete simpler tasks.

However, if you have a skill you'd like to teach, such as jewellery-making, crocheting, or even baking - you can consider offering classes to people interested in learning these skills. One of the more common ways of doing this nowadays is by showcasing your work and classes on social media.

These aren't the only routes available to you! There are also opportunities to go into the world and become a master at your skill, to the point that you are considered an expert in your field. From there you can either partner with an institution to offer classes, or even form your own online courses, that anyone can sign up for!

What truly matters most is the quality of your craft, how well you can help your students learn your skill, and how passionate you are about what you teach. As long as you are good at what you do, and people want to learn what you do, you can become a teacher.

However, let's not forget that being a teacher is more than just imparting knowledge and skills. It's about making a positive impact on the lives of others and shaping the future generation. As a teacher, you have the power to inspire, mentor, and guide students towards their full potential.

When you become a teacher, it is important to keep the mindset of being a student yourself. Constantly learn new things about your craft and new ways to teach your craft better to keep improving your teaching capabilities.

By constantly learning about your students, you get to understand which teaching styles suit them better, and you can also guide them towards being better individuals beyond what you're teaching.

So, now that you better understand what this career is about and the different ways you can be a teacher, do you feel this is a career you would like to pursue in the future? Also, remember that being a teacher is most importantly about teaching something you truly are passionate about. Is there a skill or subject you deeply connect with and want to teach to the world?

The influence you have as a teacher extends far beyond the classroom walls, as you contribute to the development of well-rounded individuals who can contribute positively to society. So, embrace the role of a teacher with passion and dedication, knowing that you have the opportunity to shape minds, ignite curiosity, and make a lasting difference in the world.

My Inspiration

Shubhi Saxena
Founder, Unibino

As a parent in this ever-changing world, it can sometimes feel overwhelming when it comes to our children's futures. New technologies seem to be arising almost every day, and with so many innovations, it creates unique professions which many of us wouldn't have dreamed to be necessary only a few years ago. Which to me is a good thing. Because with so much variety, my children can have the opportunity to pick a career that will fit their personalities and build upon their strengths. As you may imagine, this desire within me to provide my children with the resources they needed to thrive, led me to search out books that would be easy enough for them to understand while teaching them about various professions.

Only, I found that these books were few and far between. Even if I could find a book about a certain profession geared towards young readers, I found them sparse inside and limited to only certain careers that may not fit my children's abilities. This is when I came up with the idea to write my own children's books, teaching them about all the various careers in the modern world. After months of researching different professions and learning more than I ever expected, I quickly realised this was going to be a bigger project than I first anticipated. I dove into the histories of these professions, discovering links to the past, and why these professions were now so important.

Ultimately my goal was to offer my children options, to show them that there is no one set path for everyone. But in this, I stumbled upon something bigger. I wanted to share this with future generations. To share with all children and parents about these careers, to help spark curiosity, and to instil a passion for the future. Everyone has special talents and abilities, and I hope that this series will be able to offer clarity and inspiration to children around the world. Because at the end of the day, it's never too early to start dreaming and never too late to take action. With this, I hope you enjoy this series and that your young ones become the best versions of themselves as they can achieve.